Theory Workbook
Level Four
By Wesley Schaum

T0081941

Schaum's Pathway to Musicianship

The *Schaum Making Music Piano Library* integrates method, theory, technic and note reading with appealing materials for recital and repertoire. Schaum's well-proven motivational philosophy and sound pedagogy are widely recognized.

FOREWORD

This workbook presents basic music theory intended to supplement any Level Four method book and for <u>all ages</u>. Ear training and eye training are encouraged by teaching recognition of major and minor chords, major and harmonic minor scales, and syncopated rhythm patterns. Transposing by interval is developed. The scale fundamentals presented here lay the groundwork for more analytical study of scales later. <u>Scale fingerings</u> for both hands are shown separately on the back inside cover.

For most students, one workbook page can be assigned every week; in some cases two pages can be assigned together. These pages should be checked and corrected <u>before</u> the "keyboard assignment" is started. Regular <u>keyboard practice of these workbook pages is essential</u> to reinforce the learning process.

INDEX

ISBN 978-1-62906-019-4

XCLUSIVELY DISTRIBUTED BY

Schaum

HAL•LEONARD®

Visit Hal Leonard Online at
www.halleonard.com

Contact us:
Hal Leonard
7777 West Bluemound Road
Milwaukee, WI 53213
Email: info@halleonard.com

In Europe, contact:
Hal Leonard Europe Limited
42 Wigmore Street
Marylebone, London, W1U 2RN
Email: info@halleonardeurope.com

In Australia, contact:
Hal Leonard Australia Pty. Ltd.
4 Lentara Court
Cheltenham, Victoria, 3192 Australia
Email: info@halleonard.com.au

Lesson 1: Beams Connecting Notes in Two Staffs

Name_____ Date_____ Score_____

A *beam* is the heavy line which connects the stems of two or more 8th notes. A *double-beam* is used to connect two or more 16th notes.

A beam may sometimes connect notes in both the upper and lower staffs. The notes *below* the beam are to be played with the *left hand*; notes *above* the beam are played with the *right hand*.

When a beam connects notes in two staffs there are usually *no rests*. The combination of notes in *both staffs* adds up to the correct number of counts for those beats. This is shown in the sample line below.

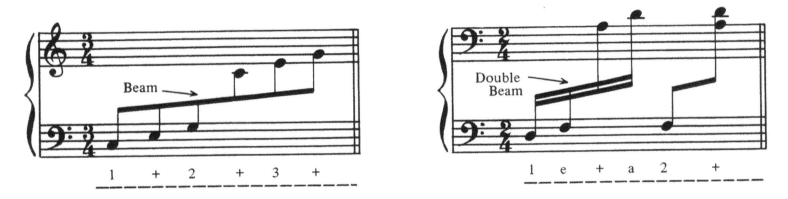

DIRECTIONS: Write the counting numbers on the dotted line below each measure. Be sure the numbers are placed *directly below* the notes.

KEYBOARD ASSIGNMENT: After completing the written work, play each measure, counting aloud as you play. Do this at least three times per day.

Lesson 2: Forming Minor Triads from Major Triads

Name_____ Date_____ Score_____

A Minor Triad is formed from a Major Triad by *lowering the third degree one half-step* as shown in the sample line below. The *chord symbol* for a minor triad has a small letter "m" added beside the chord name.

DIRECTIONS: Change the chord below each box to a *minor triad:*
1. Copy any accidentals from the major triad at the beginning of the measure.
2. Add a flat or natural sign to lower the third degree one half-step.
3. Write the chord symbol for each minor triad in the box. The first measure is a sample.

KEYBOARD ASSIGNMENT: After completing the written work, play all measures; recite the chord names ("F Major, F minor, etc.") aloud while playing. Do this at least three times per day.

TEACHERS NOTE: This lesson provides an opportunity for *ear training*. The student should be encouraged to learn the *difference in sound* between a major and minor triad.

Lesson 3: First Inversion of Major and Minor Triads

Name _____ Date _____ Score _____

To INVERT means to "turn upside down." In music, a root position triad may be inverted by moving the bottom note (root) *up one octave*; the other notes remain the same. This is called the *First Inversion*. Both major and minor triads may be inverted as shown in the sample line below.

R = Root Position   1st = First Inversion

DIRECTIONS: Write the root note in each measure to form a first inversion chord where indicated; be sure that the note is placed *one octave higher* than in root position. Draw a stem as needed; add an accidental, if necessary. The first measure is a sample.

KEYBOARD ASSIGNMENT: After completing the written work, play each measure. Recite the words "root position" or "first inversion" as each chord is played. Do this at least three times per day.

Lesson 4: Second Inversion of Triads

Name_____ Date_____ Score_____

A chord may have as many different positions as it has notes. A three-note triad has three positions:

    1. Root Position   2. First Inversion   3. Second Inversion

The SECOND INVERSION of a triad is formed by moving the bottom note of a first inversion triad *up one octave* as shown in the sample line below.

    R = Root Position   1st = First Inversion   2nd = Second Inversion

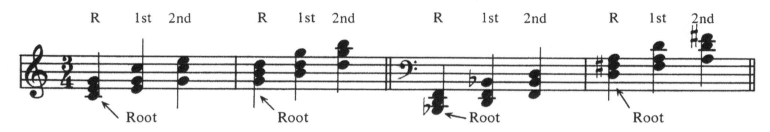

DIRECTIONS: Write notes in each measure to form a 1st and 2nd inversion chord where indicated. Draw stems and flags as needed; add accidentals, if necessary. The first measure is a sample.

KEYBOARD ASSIGNMENT: After completing the written work, play each line of music. Recite the words "root position," "first inversion," or "second inversion" as each chord is played.

TEACHERS NOTE: For training the eye to recognize the difference between 1st and 2nd inversions you may explain: 1st Inversion: Upper interval is 4th, Lower interval is 3rd.   2nd Inversion: Upper interval is 3rd, Lower interval is 4th.

Lesson 5: Three Staff and Four Staff Reading

Name _____ Date _____ Score _____

A cross-hand accompaniment which moves from bass to treble and back is sometimes written on three staffs as shown in the line below. The letters "R.H." (right hand) and "L.H." (left hand) are often written at the beginning of the first line of music. Notice that the notes in the top and bottom staffs go together to form a complete accompaniment pattern. The melody is in the center staff.

DIRECTIONS: Draw a circle around all accompaniment notes played with the left hand. Then write the counting numbers on the dotted line in each measure. The first measure is a sample.

Music with a wide range, using notes low in the bass and high in the treble staffs, is sometimes written on four staffs for ease of reading. It is not expected that you hold down the melody notes in the two bottom staffs while playing the two top staffs. The damper pedal serves to sustain the melody notes while the accompaniment chords are played in the two top staffs.

DIRECTIONS: Draw a circle around all accompaniment chords in the top two staffs. Then write the counting numbers on the dotted line in each measure.

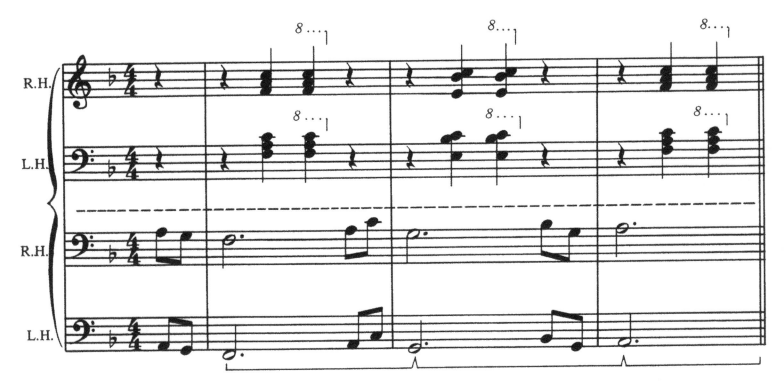

KEYBOARD ASSIGNMENT: After completing the written work, play each line of music.
Do this at least three times per day.

Lesson 6: Chained Melody Notes

Name_____Date_____Score_____

Melody notes that move between one staff and another are sometimes "chained" together with dotted lines to make the melody easier to follow. Ths is shown in sample No. 1 below.

Music with a cross-hand accompaniment may sometimes have the melody notes "chained" together with dotted lines also for ease of reading. This is shown in sample No. 2 below.

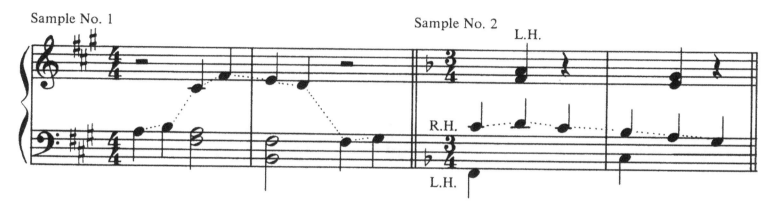

DIRECTIONS: Draw a dotted line connecting the melody notes in each line below. Refer to the samples above.

KEYBOARD ASSIGNMENT: After completing the written work, play all lines of music. Do this at least three times per day.

TEACHERS NOTE: Point out that *stem direction* often indicates the melody with a cross-hand accompaniment. A cross-hand accompaniment, as in the 6/8 line above, often has no rests; the left-hand notes when added together make the correct number of counts.

Lesson 7: Single 16th Notes and Rests

Name_____Date_____Score_____

Compare the 8th notes and 16th notes below. Notice that the 8th notes have a *single* flag, the 16th notes have a *double* flag. Likewise, an 8th rest has a *single* curve and a 16th rest has a *double* curve.

* The sample line below shows counting with various groups of 16th notes and rests.

DIRECTIONS: Draw a circle around the *single* 16th notes and 16th rests in the lines below. Then write the counting on the dotted line below each measure.

KEYBOARD ASSIGNMENT: After completing the written work, play the notes in each line using a slow to moderate tempo; count aloud as you play. Do this at least three times per day.

***TEACHERS NOTE**: Because of different ways of teaching, the counting of 16th notes has been purposely left to the preference of the teacher. As a suggestion, you could use "one-ee-and-ah" (the spoken number, of course, would depend upon the number of the beat).

Lesson 8: 16th Note Groups in 3/8, 6/8, and 9/8 Time

Name_____ Date_____ Score_____

The note and rest values are the same in 3/8, 6/8, and 9/8 time. The line below show samples of counting with different combinations of 16th notes.

Notice the *dotted quarter rest* which is counted the same as a dotted quarter note.

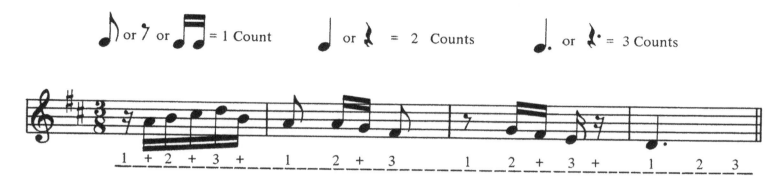

DIRECTIONS: Write the counting on the dotted line below each measure.
Watch for changes of time signature.

KEYBOARD ASSIGNMENT: After completing the written work, play each line of music; count aloud as you play. Do this at least three times per day.

Lesson 9: Phrasing

Name_____Date_____ Score_____

A *phrase* is a group of notes connected by a curved line called a *slur* or *phrase mark*. The slur may be placed over or under a group of notes and may be several measures long. Phrasing is a kind of musical punctuation similar to a comma or period in a sentence.

   *Notes within a phrase are to be played *legato*. A phrase is started by depressing a key, playing legato throughout the phrase, and releasing the key at the end of the phrase. The final note of a phrase is usually shortened slightly as indicated by a *breath mark* (,) in the sample phrases below. This mark is used in vocal music to indicate the place where a singer is to take a breath. At the keyboard, the breath mark at the end of a phrase is approximately similar to a 16th rest.

Phrases may include tied notes. This sometimes results in the phrase mark and tie ending at the same time, as shown in the sample line below.

DIRECTIONS: Draw a breath mark (,) at the end of each phrase in the lines below.

KEYBOARD ASSIGNMENT: Play each line of music. Be sure to shorten the last note of each phrase by lifting the key slightly early – about equal to a 16th rest. Do this at least three times each day.

*TEACHERS NOTE: The precise method of starting and ending a phrase (involving wrist, forearm, and elbow) is left to the personal preference of the teacher.

Lesson 10: Practical Uses of the Slur

Name_____ Date_____ Score_____

A slur or phrase mark helps guide the eye to make note reading easier. The eye should try to read the *entire group* of notes within a slur, if possible. In the line below, the slurs divide the melody into two sections.

DIRECTIONS: Draw a breath mark (**'**) at the end of each phrase or slur in the lines below (see Lesson 9)

In the line below, slurs point out broken chords and arpeggios in an accompaniment.

In the line below, slurs point out scale segments.

In the line below, slurs point out similar patterns in an accompaniment.

A short slur is sometimes used with words when two or more melody notes fit with one syllable. Notice that these short slurs fit within the longer phrases. A phrase often ends with a comma, period, or other punctuation in the lyrics.

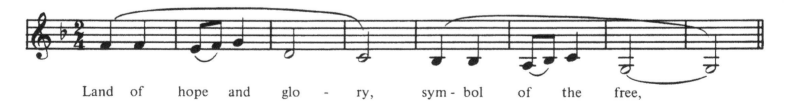

Land of hope and glo - ry, sym - bol of the free,

KEYBOARD ASSIGNMENT: Play each line of music; try to let your eye read all of the notes in each slur. Make the notes *legato* within each slur; shorten the note at the end of each slur as explained in Lesson 9. Do this at least three times per day.

TEACHERS NOTE: Point out that if the last note of a phrase gets more than one count, the breath mark should be placed where the counts are finished – just before the start of the next phrase.

The slur can also be an aid to fingering and hand position. Slurs and phrase marks can help in memorizing music by organizing the melody and accompaniment into logical groups that are more easily remembered.

Some musicians make a distinction between a phrase and a slur; the phrase being usually longer and associated with the melody.

Lesson 11: Harmonic Minor Scale Construction: A Minor and E Minor

Name_____Date_____Score_____

The most commonly used minor scale is the *harmonic* minor. It consists of eight notes in musical alphabet order; each note has a number name called a *degree*. The harmonic minor scale has a special sequence of half steps and whole steps and includes a unique wide interval of 1½ steps.

   The harmonic minor scale shown below has A as the root. Scale degree numbers are printed below each note. "H," "W," or "1½" indicates the size of the step between each scale degree.

H = Half Step   W = Whole Step   1½ = 1½ Step

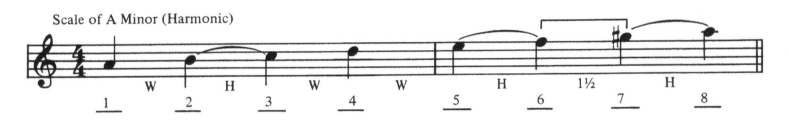

DIRECTIONS: Write the scale degree number on the line *below* each note. Then write "H," "W," or "1½" between each degree number (as in the sample line above). Add accidentals as needed to form the sequence of steps between the degrees of a harmonic minor scale in each line below. Draw a slur connecting the notes forming a *half step*; draw a square bracket above the notes forming the 1½ step (as in sample).

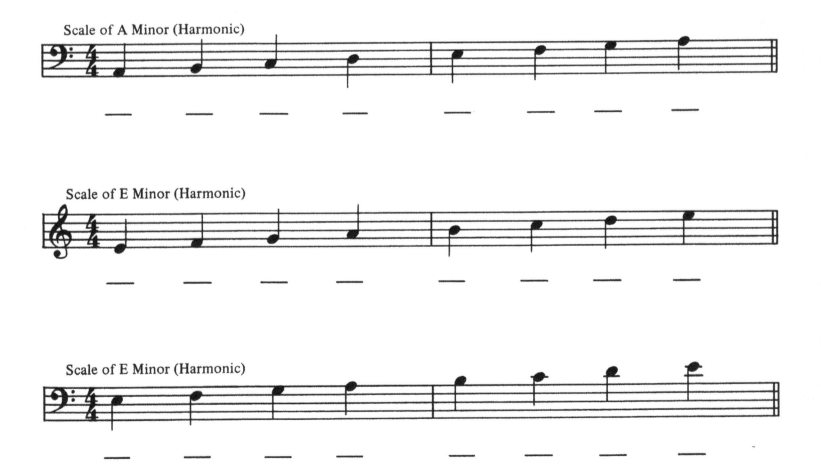

KEYBOARD ASSIGNMENT: After completing the written work, play the A minor and E minor scales with each hand; use the fingering shown on page 32. Do this at least three times per day.

TEACHERS NOTE: It is recommended that the student be *at the keyboard* when doing the written work on this page.

Lesson 12: Harmonic Minor Scales: B, D, and G Minor

Name_____ Date_____ Score_____

The harmonic minor scale shown below has B as the root. Scale degree numbers are printed below each note.

      H = Half Step   W = Whole Step   1½ = 1½ Step

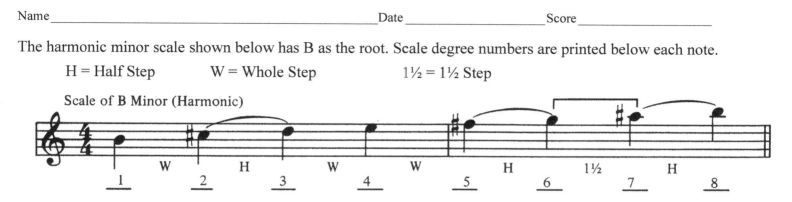

DIRECTIONS: Write the scale degree number on the line *below* each note. Then write "H," "W," or "1½" between each degree number (as in the sample line above). Add accidentals as needed to form the sequence of steps between the degrees of a harmonic minor scale in each line below. Draw a slur connecting the notes forming a *half step*; draw a square bracket above the notes forming the 1½ step (as in sample).

KEYBOARD ASSIGNMENT: After completing the written work, play the B, D, and G minor scales with each hand; use the fingering shown on page 32. Do this at least three times per day.

TEACHERS NOTE: It is recommended that the student be *at the keyboard* when doing the written work on this page.

Lesson 13: Relative Minor

Name_____ Date_____ Score_____

Every major scale has a relative harmonic minor scale. They are related because they have the *same key signature*. The root of the relative minor scale is the sixth degree of the relative major as shown in the sample line below.

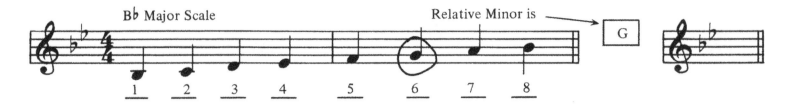

DIRECTIONS: The lines below contain various major scales. Write numbers for the scale degree on the line below each note; draw a circle around the note which is the *6th degree* of each major scale. Then write the letter name of the root of the relative minor scale in the box and write the key signature in the measure that follows. The line above is a sample.

Lesson 14: Identifying Major and Minor Key Signatures

Name_____ Date _____ Score _____

There are two ways to help determine if a key signature is major or minor.

      1. Listen to the music: A *major* key usually sounds happy, cheerful, and bright.

                                 A *minor* key usually sounds sad, mysterious, or spooky.

      2. Analyze the last two measures of a piece, looking for the root.

        * The root is usually the bottom note (in bass clef) at the end of a piece.

      Sometimes the root is also the last top note (in treble clef). This is shown in the sample line below.

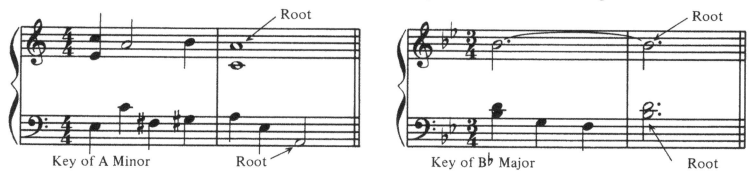

DIRECTIONS: Look at the last bottom note and last top note in each pair of measures below. Compare these to the key signature to determine if the key is major or minor. (Consult Lesson 13, if necessary). Write the letter name and the word "major' or "minor" on the blank line below each final measure.

*TEACHERS NOTE: Point out that the root guidelines explained here will find the key in a majority of pieces. There are, of course, exceptions which will require more emphasis on the listening aspect of key determination.

Lesson 15: D.C. al fine and D.S. al fine

Name_____ Date_____ Score_____

D.C. al fine and *D.S. al fine* are abbreviations which are nearly the same.
The important difference is in the second letter of each: "**D.C.**" and "**D.S.**"

D.C. al fine = da **capo** al fine (dah KAH-poh ahl FEE-nay)

It means to return to the **beginning** of the piece and repeat, ending at the word *fine* (fine = end or finish).

D.S. al fine = dal **segno** al fine (dahl SEN-yo ahl FEE-nay).

It means to return to the **sign** (𝄋) and repeat, ending at the word *fine*. The "sign" resembles a dollar sign.

DIRECTIONS: Draw a circle around the letter "C" or letter "S" in each abbreviation. Then write the word "beginning" or draw the "sign" on each blank line.

D.C. al fine =
return to the _____

D.S. al fine =
return to the _____

D.S. al fine =
return to the _____

D.C. al fine =
return to the _____

KEYBOARD ASSIGNMENT: Circle the word "fine" in the music. Then play the music, observing the *D.S. al fine*. Do this once each day.

D.S. al fine

Lesson 16: White Key Sharps and Flats

Name_____ Date_____ Score_____

The SHARP means to go UP *one half-step*. In most cases this is a black key. However, B sharp and E sharp are "white key sharps" because one half-step up from B or E is a *white key*.

The FLAT means to go DOWN *one half-step*. This is usually a black key. C flat and F flat are "white key flats" because one half-step down from C or F is a *white key*. This is shown on the keyboard charts below.

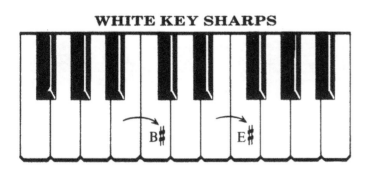

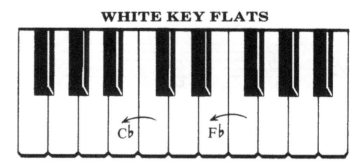

DIRECTIONS: Draw a circle around the notes which are white key sharps or flats. Then write the letter of the white key above each circle.

KEYBOARD ASSIGNMENT: After completing the written work, play all of the white key sharps and flats. Do this at least three times per day.

TEACHERS NOTE: Enharmonic relationships are presented later in Lesson 30.

Lesson 17: Forming 6th Chords from Major Triads

Name_____ Date_____ Score_____

* A Sixth Chord has *four notes*. The name, sixth, is used because the interval from the root to the top note is a 6th. The top note is also the 6th degree of the major scale (where the root of the chord is the 1st degree).

A 6th chord is formed by adding the 6th degree of the major scale above a root position major triad.

The sample line below shows major triads followed by a sixth chord with the same root. Notice that the *chord symbol* has the number "6" added to the chord name.

DIRECTIONS: Change the chord below each box to form a 6th chord:

1. Copy any accidentals from the major triad at the beginning of each measure.
2. Write a note which forms the interval of a 6th above the root.
   (All notes will have to be written on the *right side* of the stem)
3. The note you write must be *one whole step* above the top note of each major triad.
   (You may have to add a sharp or flat sign to spell the 6th correctly.)
4. Write the chord symbol for each 6th chord in the box. The first measure is a sample.

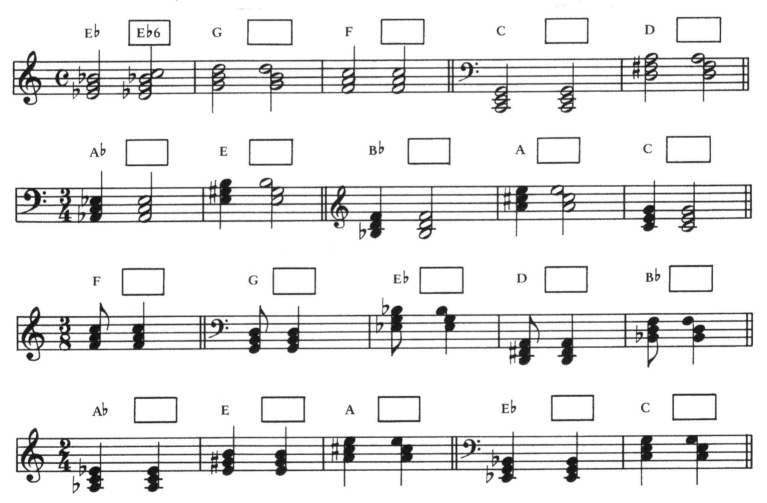

KEYBOARD ASSIGNMENT: After completing the written work, play all measures; recite the chord names ("F Major, F Six, etc.") aloud while playing Do this at least three times per day.

*TEACHERS NOTE: The 6th chord taught here is the same as found in standard chord symbols. You may also explain that the top note of a 6th chord is *one whole step* above the top note of a root position major triad.

This lesson provides an opportunity for *ear training*. The student should be encouraged to learn the *difference in sound* between a major triad and a 6th chord.

Lesson 18: Forming 7th Chords from Major Triads

Name_____ Date_____ Score_____

* A Seventh Chord has *four notes*. The name, seventh, is used because the intrval from the root to the top note is a 7th.

A 7th chord is formed by taking the 7th degree of the major scale, lowering it one half step, and adding it above a root position major triad. (Where the root of the chord is the 1st degree of the scale).

The sample line below shows major triads followed by a seventh chord with the same root. Notice that the *chord symbol* has the number "7" added to the chord name.

DIRECTIONS: Change the chord below each box to form a 7th chord:

1. Copy any accidentals from the major triad at the beginning of each measure.
2. Write a note which forms the interval of a 7th above the root.
3. The note you write must be three *half steps* above the top note of each major triad.
   (You may have to add a flat sign to spell the 7th correctly.)
4. Write the chord symbol for each 7th chord in the box. The first measure is a sample.

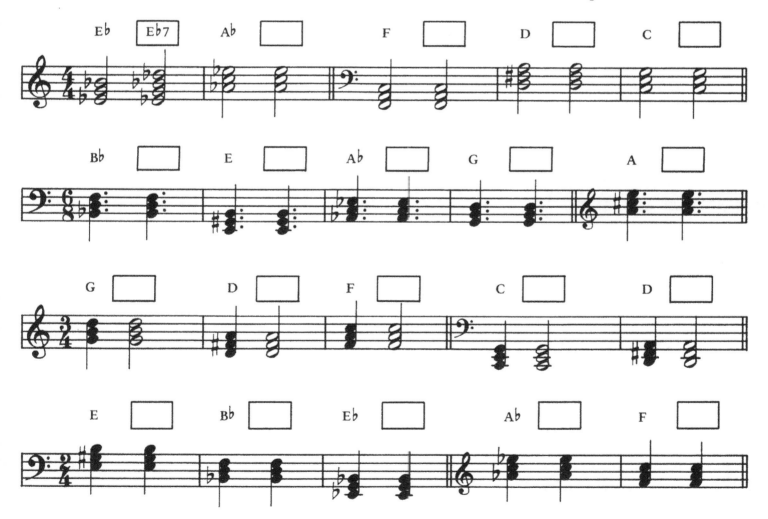

KEYBOARD ASSIGNMENT: After completing the written work, play all measures; recite the chord names ("F Major, F Seven, etc.") aloud while playing. Do this at least three times per day.

*TEACHERS NOTE: The 7th chord taught here is the same as found in standard chord symbols. This lesson provides an opportunity for *ear training*. The student should be encouraged to learn the *difference in sound* between a major triad and a 7th chord.

Lesson 19: Transposing by Interval: Major Keys

Name_____ Date_____ Score_____

To transpose a melody means to play it in a *different key*, starting on a higher or lower note. When transposing by interval you look for movement, up or down. For example, if the melody moves up a 4th, the transposed version will also move up a 4th.

The two sample lines below show the same melody in the key of F major and G major. Interval numbers have been written between notes.

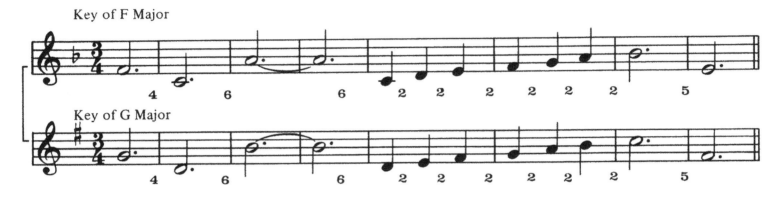

DIRECTIONS: The line below is a B-flat major melody with interval numbers written between the notes. In the second line, write notes to transpose the melody to C major. The starting note is printed. If necessary, write the interval numbers between notes below the second line.

DIRECTIONS: The line below is a G major melody. Write the interval numbers between notes below the first line. In the second line, write notes to transpose the melody to D major. The starting note is printed. If necessary, write the interval numbers between notes below the second line.

KEYBOARD ASSIGNMENT: After completing the written work, play each line of music. Do this at least three times per day.

TEACHERS NOTE: Point out that the practical reasons for transposing are to play with an instrument pitched in a different key (such as trumpet or saxophone) and to adjust an accompaniment to a different vocal range.

Lesson 20: Transposing by Interval: Minor Keys

Name_____ Date_____ Score_____

DIRECTIONS: The line below is a G minor melody with interval numbers written between the notes. In the second line, write notes to transpose the melody to A minor. The starting note is printed. If necessary, write the interval numbers between notes below the second line.

DIRECTIONS: Write the interval numbers between notes in the E minor melody below. In the second line, write notes to transpose the melody to B minor. The starting note is printed. If necessary, write the interval numbers between notes below the second line.

DIRECTIONS: Write the interval numbers between notes in the D minor melody below. In the second line, write notes to transpose the melody to E minor. The starting note is printed. If necessary, write the interval numbers between notes below the second line.

KEYBOARD ASSIGNMENT: After completing the written work, play each line of music. Do this at least three times per day.

TEACHER'S NOTE: It may be helpful to do this lesson at the keyboard. Transposing with accidentals is presented later in Lesson 31.

Lesson 21: Polyphonic Music

Name_____ Date_____ Score_____

Polyphonic music has *two or more* melodies played at the same time that blend together harmoniously, usually without any accompaniment. *Polyphonic* means literally "many sounds." Pachelbel's "Canon" is a familiar example of polyphonic music.

A *round* is a kind of polyphonic music where the same melody is started at different times, overlapping and sounding simultaneously. "Frere Jacques" and "Row, Row, Row Your Boat" are familiar rounds.

DIRECTIONS: The melody in the treble clef, "Sweetly Sings the Donkey," is written as one part of a *round*. Write the notes for the second part of the round one octave lower in the bass clef (the second part is started in the 5th measure). Notice that the first part starts alone and the second part ends alone.

KEYBOARD ASSIGNMENT: After completing the written work, play both parts of the round together. Do this at least once per day.

TEACHER'S NOTE: Explanation of this added information is optional. *Monophonic music* has a single melody with accompaniment.

Counterpoint is another name often given to polyphonic music. A *canon* is a strict form of polyphonic music resembling a round, but requiring exact imitation whenever the melody appears.

Lesson 22: Two-Voice Rhythms

Name_____ Date_____ Score_____

Some music may have the melody or accompaniment divided into two parts in the same staff. This is usually indicated by stem direction: *stems up* for the upper part, *stems down* for the lower part, as shown in the line below.

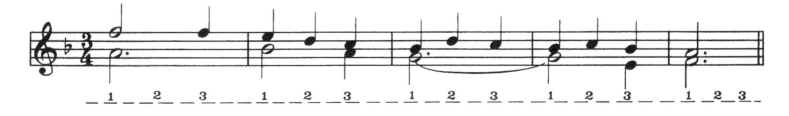

Each part, or *voice*, has its own independent counting with rests as needed for the correct number of beats in each measure. This may result in two sets of rests in the same staff (for the upper and lower voices) as shown in the line below.

DIRECTIONS: Write the counting numbers on the dotted line below each measure. Then draw rests as needed to make a complete number of counts for both upper and lower voices in each line below. It may be necessary to place rests a little higher or lower than the usual position in the staff.

KEYBOARD ASSIGNMENT: After completing the written work, play each line of music at a slow to moderate tempo. Count aloud as you play. Do this at least two times per day.

Lesson 23: Cut Time (2/2)

Name_____Date_____ Score_____

"Cut time" is a common name given to the 2/2 time signature. There are two counts per measure. A *half note* gets one count. The symbol for cut time is (𝄵). It is also sometimes called *alla breve*.

Note values are as follows:

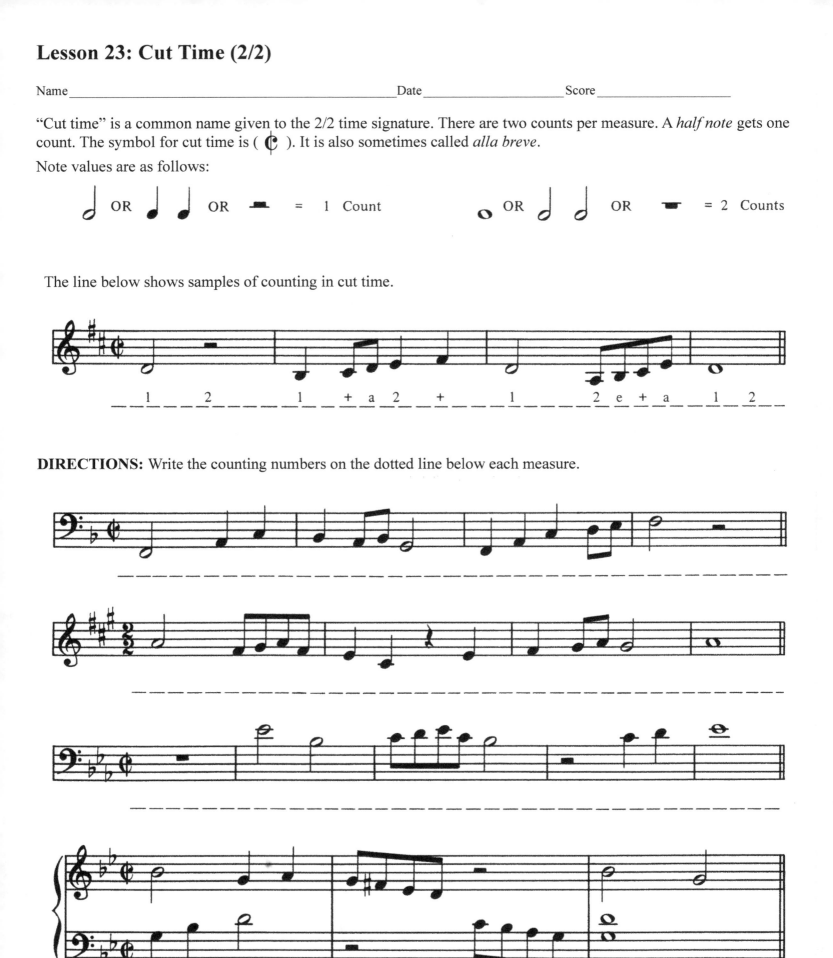

The line below shows samples of counting in cut time.

DIRECTIONS: Write the counting numbers on the dotted line below each measure.

KEYBOARD ASSIGNMENT: After completing the written work, play each line of music. Count aloud as you play. Do this at least two times per day.

TEACHER'S NOTE: For some students, it may be helpful to add a "+" after *every* numbered count. Explain that in cut time, 8th notes are counted the same as 16th notes in 4/4 time.

Lesson 24: 3/2 Time Signature

Name_____ Date_____ Score_____

In 3/2 time there are *three counts* per measure. The note values are the same as in *cut time* (see Lesson 23). The line below shows samples of counting in 3/2 time.

            1   2   3   1   2   + a 3 +   1   2   + 3   +   1   2   3

DIRECTIONS: Write the counting numbers on the dotted line below each measure.

DIRECTIONS: Add rests as needed to make three complete counts in each measure. Then write the counting numbers on the dotted line below each measure.

KEYBOARD ASSIGNMENT: After completing the written work, play each line of music; count aloud as you play. Do this at least three times per day.

Lesson 25: D-Flat and G-Flat Major Scales

Name_____ Date_____ Score_____

Notes of the D-flat Major Scale are shown below with scale degree numbers. The letter H shows the location of the two *Half Steps*. All other steps are *Whole Steps*.

DIRECTIONS: Add flats where necessary to make the pattern of whole steps and half steps for the D-flat Major Scale in both staffs. Write letter names, including the necessary flat, in the box below each note.

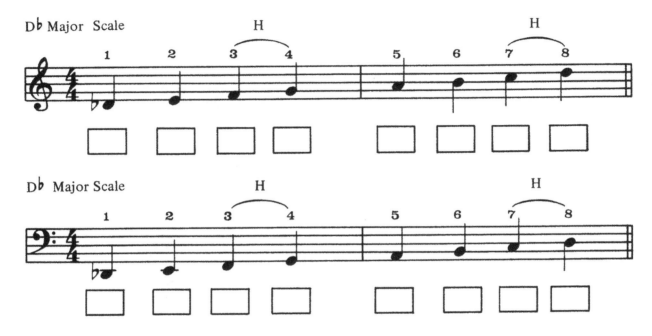

Notes of the G-flat Major Scale are shown below with scale degree numbers. The letter H shows the location of the two *Half Steps*. All other steps are *Whole Steps*.

DIRECTIONS: Add flats where necessary to make the pattern of whole steps and half steps for the G-flat Major Scale in both staffs. Write letter names, including the necessary flat, in the box below each note.

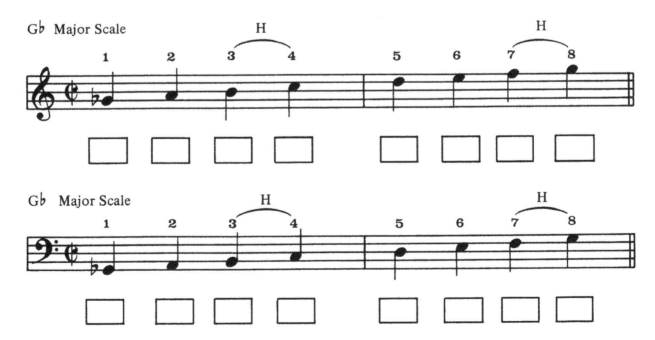

KEYBOARD ASSIGNMENT: After completing the written work, play both scales with each hand using the fingering shown on page 32. Do this at least three times per day.

TEACHER'S NOTE: It is recommended that the student be *at the keyboard* when doing the written work on this page. Be sure the student places the flat sign *before* a note and *after* a letter name.

Lesson 26: Key Signature Changes: Major and Minor

Name_____ Date_____ Score_____

A change of key signature is preceded by a double bar. When necessary, one or more natural signs are used to cancel all or part of the previous key signature. The line below shows samples of three different key singature changes.

Key of __A__ Major   Key of __F__ Major   Key of __Ab__ Major   Key of __G__ Minor   Key of __B__ Minor   Key of __C__ Major

DIRECTIONS: Write the letter name for each key signature above each measure. Notice that some signatures are labeled major, others are minor. If necessary, refer to the front inside cover for key signature names.

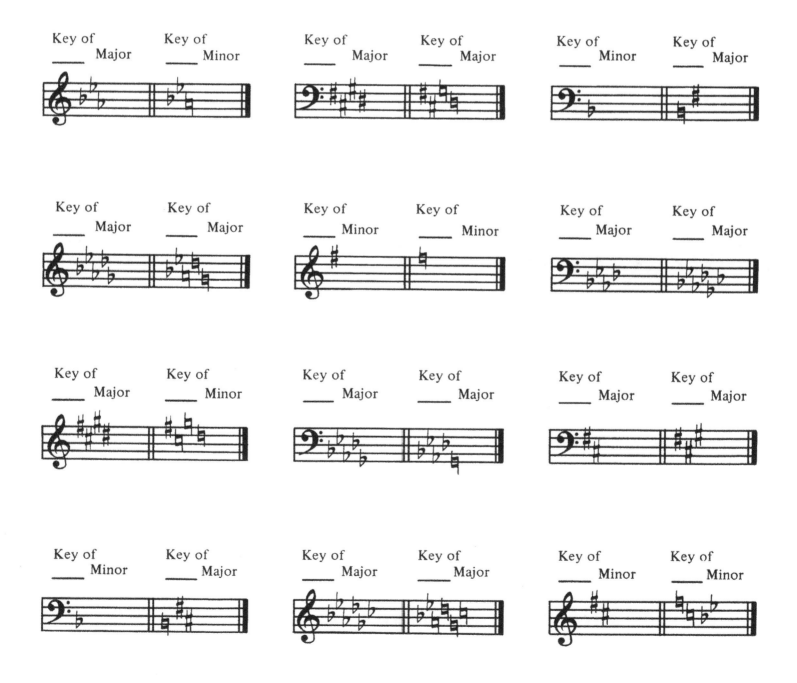

Lesson 27: Recognizing Syncopated Rhythms

Name_____Date_____Score_____

Many syncopated rhythms are easy to recognize by looking for special note groups. Common syncopations begin with a single 8th note or with an 8th note tied to another note.

In the samples below, there is a bracket printed above each syncopated note group.

A small accent mark (–) is printed above the syncopated note in each group.

Counting of these syncopations is shown in the sample line below.

DIRECTIONS: Write the counting numbers on the dotted line below each measure. Draw a bracket above each group of syncopated notes; then add a small accent mark (–) above the syncopated note in each group.

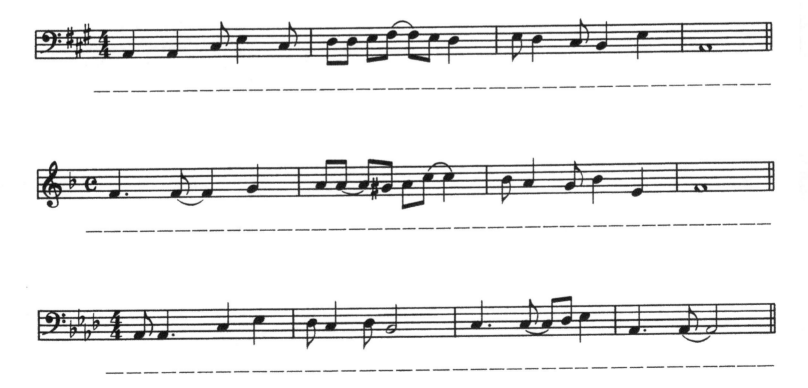

KEYBOARD ASSIGNMENT: After completing the written work, play each line of music, counting aloud as you play. Do this at least three times per day.

TEACHER'S NOTE: The student's eye should be trained to recognize the syncopated groups shown at the top of this page.

Lesson 28: 12/8 Time Signature

Name_____Date_____Score_____

In 12/8 time there are 12 counts per measure; an *8th note* gets one count. Note values are as follows:

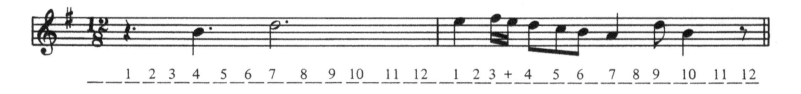

The line below shows samples of counting in 12/8 time.

DIRECTIONS: Write the counting numbers on the dotted line below each measure.

DIRECTIONS: Write the counting numbers on the dotted line below each measure. Then add rests as needed to make 12 counts in each measure.

KEYBOARD ASSIGNMENT: After completing the written work, play each line of music. Count aloud as you play. Do this at least two times per day.

TEACHER'S NOTE: In 12/8 time, it is often easier for the student to think of four main beats in each measure (one for every three counts) instead of trying to count all twelve numbers. Metronome marks for 12/8 time usually indicate a dotted quarter note gets one beat.

Lesson 29: Double-Sharps and Double-Flats

Name_____ Date_____ Score_____

A *double-sharp* (✗) is a symbol indicating that a note is to be *raised two half-steps*. This usually results in a "white key sharp." For example, F double-sharp is played as the white key, G.

A *double-flat* (♭♭) indicates that a note is to be *lowered two half steps*. The result is usually a "white key flat." For example, B double-flat is played as the white key, A. This is shown in the keyboard diagrams below.

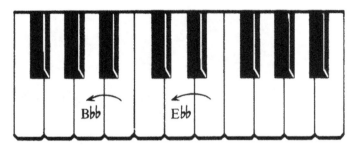 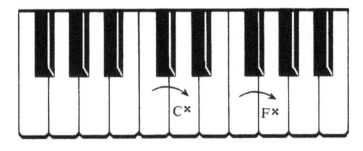

When a double-sharped note is changed to a single sharp, the double-sharp is cancelled by a natural sign, followed by a single sharp. Similarly, when a double-flatted note is changed to a single flat, the double-flat is cancelled by a natural sign, followed by a single flat.

Double-sharps and double-flats are necessary to spell scales and chords correctly, especially where the key signature has four or more sharps or flats.

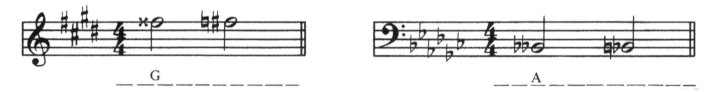

DIRECTIONS: Draw a circle around all double-sharps and double-flats in each line below. On the dotted line below, write the letter name of the *white key* that is the same as the double-sharp or double-flat.

KEYBOARD ASSIGNMENT: After completing the written work, play each line of music, watching especially for double-sharps and double-flats. Do this at least three times per day.

TEACHER'S NOTE: Point out that when a double-sharp is used with a note which has been previously sharp, the double-sharp *replaces* the single sharp. (The double-sharp is *not added* to the single sharp.) Likewise, a double-flat is *not added* to a note previously flat.

A *single* natural sign cancels a double-sharp and double-flat. A double natural sign is *not needed* although it is occasionally found in some music.

Lesson 30: Enharmonic Notes

Name_____ Date_____ Score_____

Enharmonic means the same musical pitch written in different ways, such as C# and D-flat. White key sharps and flats, double-sharps, and double-flats are also included in enharmonic spellings. Each measure of the sample line below has two different spellings of the same pitch.

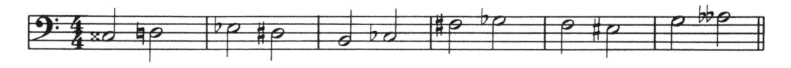

DIRECTIONS: Add an accidental to the *second note* in each measure to make it *enharmonic* to the first note. The added accidental may have to be double-sharp or a double-flat. If the second note needs to change, just add a *natural sign*.

KEYBOARD ASSIGNMENT: After completing the written work, play each line of music. Do this at least three times per day.

TEACHER'S NOTE: This lesson should be done at the keyboard. Explain that enharmonic notes are like homonymns (words that sound alike but are spelled differently) such as "to, too and two." An easy way to draw a double-sharp is simply an "X."

This lesson is an opportunity for ear and eye training: recognizing enharmonic notes that sound the same.

Lesson 31: Transposing with Accidentals

Name_____ Date_____ Score_____

When transposing, the same accidental sharp, flat, or natural is often used again in the transposed key. However, depending on the new key signature, a *different* accidental may take its place. Remember:

      a SHARP *raises* the note one half-step;   a FLAT *lowers* the note one half-step

      a *NATURAL may alter the note *up or down*, depending on the previous key signature or accidental.

The three sample staffs below show a D major melody transposed to A major in the 2nd staff and E-flat major in the 3rd staff. Arrows point out the accidentals Notice that in the 2nd staff, the accidentals are the same as the 1st staff, although a white key sharp is needed. In the 3rd staff, natural signs and a double-flat are needed.

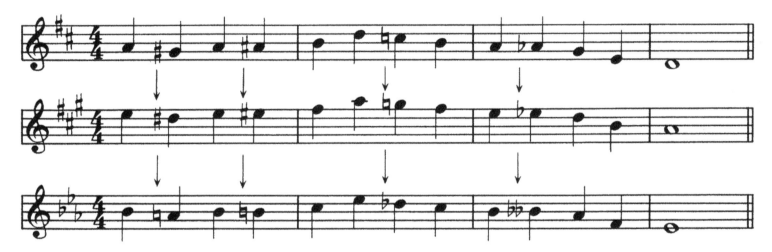

DIRECTIONS: The first staff below is an F major melody. In the second staff, add accidentals to transpose the melody to E-flat major. Draw arrows connecting the accidentals in both staffs.

DIRECTIONS: The first staff below is a B-flat major melody. In the second staff, add accidentals as needed to transpose the melody to C major. Draw arrows connecting the accidentals in both staffs.

KEYBOARD ASSIGNMENT: After completing the written work, play each line of music. Do this at least twice per day.

*TEACHER'S NOTE: Point out that a natural sign alters a pitch one *half-step* if the previous accidental is a sharp or a flat. A natural alters a pitch one *whole step* if the previous accidental is a double-sharp or double-flat.

    The final test of the transposing is the ear; does the transposed version *sound right?*